AF230080

The poems in *Lexicon of the Body* are grounded in the physical experiences of intimacy and separation, perpetual change and transformation. Sometimes quiet, sometimes fierce, and always direct, these poems dive into the deep end of the ordinary joys and the big questions of a human life lived through the body and the senses.

In these poems, relationships of all kinds come together, unfold, and fall apart. Children and lovers, parents and spouses, as well as pets, gardens, and a love for the earth and the landscape invite the reader into a world both private and particular, and yet deeply universal. Exploring themes of desire and gratitude, as well as disappointment and loss, the focus rests upon honesty and authenticity.

In *Lexicon of the Body* by DM Wallace, we are reminded that the beauty and wonder of the human body binds us all together. While we think of our forms as private and precious only to us, through them we learn empathy, wisdom, and a sense of belonging to each other that transcends language.

LEXICON
OF THE BODY

LEXICON OF THE BODY

---

poems

DM WALLACE

atmosphere press

© 2022 DM (Denise) Wallace

Published by Atmosphere Press

Cover design by Ronaldo Alves
Cover art by Judith Sparks

No part of this book may be reproduced without permission from the author except in brief quotations and in reviews.

Atmospherepress.com

This book is dedicated to
my family and my husband
Jeffery V. Passerotti

Contents

IV

I

Lexicon of the Body

On a cold day, see your breath
as it escapes in white puffs
in front of your face:
the sight of your essence
free to go its own way
with no particular
attachment to you.

Could you stop it
or would you even try,
clinging to that air
at the risk of your life,
blind to how the breath
is fulfilled by itself and yet
happy to pull you along.

We believe we inhabit
our bodies so completely
but they are not really *ours,*
speaking a deeply personal
language that only belongs
to the spiral of time and the
borrowed intimacy of flesh.

Exquisite Agony

all of my body charged
clear through, a blue fire
flooding my bloodstream,
my heart flower waking up,
that thrum of sweet love flowing.

That is what we call this—
sweet love, but it is *everything:*
the wanting, the taking, the having,
when all else demands we let go.

My muscle fibers sing it,
and my bones answer back
yes, bring it on, bring it full.

My mouth wishes to be planted
with you, your actual body
becoming part of mine,

in passion, in time.

Poem to My Right Leg

Born a leader, you have
been made a follower,
trying to keep up
and barely succeeding.

Slew footed and self
conscious to a fault,
you're the one that
takes a break first.

You'd be better off
standing on your own,
and resent the left leg
in all its strength.

When I step back it is
always with you because
I know your tendency
for small considerations.

Your foot is conscripted
to the gas pedal, pushing
ahead tirelessly on its
cocked and soft heel.

Likewise, the arabesque
would be impossible
without you, a rudder
pointing toward the past.

On balance, you make
my body whole, perform
a trick of air and beauty
that reveals a loyal soul.

My Breasts Want to Please You

to sit easily in your hands
and feel protected by your desire,
by your will to master their form,
your fingers free and moving
to know all, and knowing all,
loving all.

My breasts want you to have them
to hold like fresh fruit warmed
and ripening in morning sun,
your hands cupping each one,
your lips soft and eager
at the nipples, now sweet
and tight like blackberries.

My breasts want to comfort you,
to make a place for your head
to be healed of worry, to be
fed what your spirit craves:
this soft and supple answer
to your search for grace,
my desire unfolding.

Song for My Tongue

How deftly you relax
wet and ready for speech
behind my sharp teeth.
You are a slave to wanting,
to pleasures taken,
and pleasures given,
generous and greedy too.
A sweet snake you are
with amazing powers:
to name
and to taste
in one breath.

Ultrasound Odalisque

A hard to read mammogram
has brought me to this cool
almost dark room, a narrow bed
set among machines and blinking
lights, the whir of a computer.

I am asked to take my left arm
over my head and roll slightly
to the right, a position I offer
to my lover, or to sleep,
and now to this skilled technician.

She barely looks at me, but focuses
on computer images made of
shadow, sound waves echoing
off my dense tissues that reveal
edges and outlines of concern.

At ease in this angle of repose
and languor, I rise up and embrace
the beauties of a more romantic
era, my breasts pink and shy,
offered up for the sake of art.

The wand slides easy and impersonal
over my breast, the nipple rising straight
up to the ceiling in piqued attention if not
arousal, my whole being overwhelmed
with the desire to live.

Psychic Surgery

I startle awake as from a bad dream,
then cool relief floods over me:
something has been cut away.

A old ache, heavy and familiar
and long shrouded within me
is completely missing, but not missed.

I struggle to locate my old disease
but find it simply gone. I float free
without hope, without fear.

My new body is sweet and smooth,
light and wildly free at the very core,
weighted only by my love for this world.

Sieves

The sun is a bird that rises
on it very own schedule.
Immediate tasks are at hand
and my hands take flight,
bean picking, berry washing,
knocking slugs off the deck.

The hands that climb trees
are sticky with sap, one drop
of maple syrup draws
a circle of ants. There are
bee stings to be cleaned,
a thorn to be drawn out
backward from the wound.

Insects and simple sugars,
dirt, a fingernail, our bodies
become sieves for everything
that matters, matter itself
bleeding, mutable, beautiful.

Wildflower seeds scatter
on a hot wind. Even the clouds
have somewhere to go,
disappearing deliberately
toward the South.

Birds rule the air, absolutely.

My Boy
for Dashiell

My thinking is punctuated
by the sound my boy makes
sucking. Awake or not
it doesn't matter, his mouth
nurses his tongue even in sleep.

I love him like a wild pony,
work to break him, and hope
I don't. I dress him like a gypsy
so the wind won't take him away
while I sleep so sound in the next room.

I can't remember or reconstruct
the pain he made when he
inched out of me well done
and beautifully blue, a pearl
as pink as abalone and beautiful.

August
for Julian

Month of shooting stars
and you sit inside me, rising
beneath my blouse, shifting
but refusing to break out
into my life, my body so big
now beside your brother's
cool blue kiddie pool,
the air alive with crickets.
Sitting upside down
inside me you surround
me, your sweet butt
growing up beneath
my sternum, pressing me
with questions of
your sex, a mystery
to me, your name
a crystal I examine
in every light, never
completely sure of the
hue that is there, shifting
as you shift, opening
my eyes each morning
long after I feel you there
inside, a dream becoming.

Boy and boy, I welcome
him as I did the first
and yet anew I mother a son,
another one with a sex
unlike my own emerging
from within me.
Awe and awakening.
I lie still listening to
breathing, the breeze
on the screen,
the branches sliding
over the roof as this
child swam from me.

Opening and closing,
but still on the threshold
I stay poised, this boy
sleeping away the days,
days that are shortening
and roping us in for
the Fall. My whole
Summer was wished
away waiting for him,
and now arrived
the season changes.

Against Industrial Birth

*The Cesarean Section is the most commonly
performed unnecessary procedure in the
American medical profession.*

Every day a woman waits
for a baby is like a month
waiting for letters from home
that never come—no new family
yet, but the shadow of one at each
turn of her head, the new sway
of her hips, and the constant
swimming toward,

toward the knife, the clock
and the eager surgeon on the far
bank who decides the swimmer
has arrived although she remains
offshore, floating by holding
her breath.

As her old family seems fleeting
so she want to depart from this test
through a mist, feeling that her own
light is rising up, burning out of her
sex, singular and slow and should
be put down, put out.

How many have been scissored
in these shallow waters never
to push out the truth, the children
make the perfect shape and size
for their cave's secret passageway,
to shudder and bring forth
in the way of ecstasy,

and knowledge. Knowing as well
as wisdom is involved here,
a pleasure in the agony of waiting
that is essential: the small head
between a woman's legs
after the slow, hard work.

The Jewel

As silent as a fire
just beginning, soft brown
moles came to my skin,
scattered themselves over
my belly, my arms, my neck.
One arose close to my navel
small and jewel like in the
crown of my first pregnancy.
And the second time, another,
lighter, but close beside
like the next bead
in a string.

As silent as the house where
children sleep in their own beds
I sit at the kitchen table
counting my blessings, making
fun of my coupon box, making
eyes at my husband who touches
my new mole with his fingertip
and talks about the brightness
of the Spring moon, waxing.

As silent as conception itself
my body grew open to children,
my own willingness to change
and become the mother light,
the full moon rising slowly
and balloon like from the horizon
of myself, my own needs falling
away to reveal whole new planets
of desire, like the new moles that
bejewel my belly, my children
with their mark on me forever.

After the Flu

Since my life force fell flat
then rose back up again,
I stand in awe of my own chi
as if it were a great old tree
erupting from within me.

Stripped of Ego, Eros, my body
vanished into a vacuum and was
taken deep inside the mystery,
floundering without attitude
or attachment to anything.

Billowing upward and fed
on fire, this tree survived
and now astonishes me, rising
from the roots of my being
easy as laughter or ecstasy.

I reenter and remake
this body I inhabit, of me
and not of me, a creature
born of smoke and prayer,
my flesh newer, lighter.

II

Love Poem for Jacques Cousteau
6/11/1910—6/25/1997

As a girl I fell hard for you,
those skinny legs, that red cap.
Landlocked, a child of the desert,
I heard your lilting French English
as the voice of the sea herself.

In my dreams of sea voyage
you were always the captain,
spreading out a map, or watching
hawklike the edge of the known
world rising and falling away.

To the wind your aquiline nose
made a fine keel cutting through air,
sharp on the scent of water mammals,
whales and dolphins who still
call your name: *Cousteau.*

I felt safe diving with you
as you descended into the blue,
a child again in your well taught
diver's body, regressing in age
and reborn in an undersea garden.

Your hands were graceful
stroking the waving grasses
and darting fish, your eyes
wide with wonder and dismay
in your small oval mask.

Wrapped in the cold and squeezing
pressure of depth, your camera created
light in that underworld, taught me
to trust in letting go, in dropping
fearlessly into the deep.

All the Men I Know

need to cry and do,
as if their lives depended,
their wounds opening soft
and wide as my own sex,
wet with longing as they are
with sorrow. With the gift
of my kind I make a window
or a mirror. I come to imagine
I carry some cruel but necessary
wand within me, a sword which
opens and reopens their oldest,
deepest fear. In the harsh light
of their grief I disappear
and for a brief time find my
own release, just listening
as a shell listens to the sea,
a small bird to the wind.
I hover cool and sexless
over these lovers
and loved who need
to cry, for their kind.

Desire Pushes Us

After wandering and fasting
even the Buddha came home
to the needs of his body, his belly
growing round and full, shining
like a full moon for all to see.

See how the bumblebee
wallows in the pollen cup
of each flower, disappears
into the deepest blossoms
and emerges coated in gold.

Oceans expand and then recede,
the wind will not be denied.
Wild creatures are food for other
wild creatures, lolling in the sun,
picking meat from their teeth.

We too deserve to be satiated
at the breast of our longings,
to languish and receive
the blessings of our flesh,
our mortal pleasures taken.

A Good Map

> *…we love to contemplate blue,*
> *not because it advances to us,*
> *but because it draws us after it.*
>   Goethe's Color Theory

When I think of you, I see blue
and black, and bits of white,
such as whitecaps churned up
from the sea, momentary, free.
I believed you needed me like
a good map, more accurate than
those cheap ones we leafed through
on that bed that was really the floor.
We were both taught that sea level
is always the same, that islands
in straits retain their shapes
constantly, that waves are born
far out at sea. I fell for your
fingertips, those topographic
miniatures pushing oil paint
the color of dark water over
canvas, mapping every inch
of me. Our passion widened
like a river's mouth, changed
shape before our eyes
so we were surprised
when love's terrain divided
the clouds, leaving the sky
too blue to look at.

Provincetown

The harbors' green light
is the queen of the night,
her steady pulse piercing
the dark. A white haired
woman comes from her well
lit home, asks me if I've seen
her dog, explains the animal's
habit: how when someone leaves
the gate open, she's gone.
I wish I came bearing her dog,
or really that I was the Dachshund,
close to the ground, my own nose
burning through this narrow
street down to the sea,
and this old woman
come to find me.
In my filial bed I lie
down, bury my head
and let my child nurse
until sleeps takes him,
my nipple caught and
fluttering against the neat
roof of his new mouth.
I can still hear her calling
her dog's name into the
thinning night, singing
Bertie, Bertie, Bertie,
a keening that rides
the lashing wind missing
only the soft ears
of her wayward friend,
wandering the green
and fishy sands
untouched.

Clouds

Elvis, and my mother too,
believed we can all dissipate clouds
with our minds. Even I watch them
billow overhead, a kind of
reverence for myself. I study
the shadow of my lover on the
speeding landscape, realize
relativity in the simple fact
that we're traveling as fast
or faster than the clouds themselves,
leaving Cape Cod a thousand miles
behind us. But clouds are each
others' shadow, one with each
other, knowing nothing of
subdivisions, heavy machinery,
the picturesque and domed
silos that rise and recede in
our exhausted vapor. The freeway
coughs up farms, deepest greens
and wild spring flowers tickling
old mares knee deep in thistle.
Cows in the distance are black rocks
dotting the hillside while the smell
of pigs and pigheaded country
music coaxes me in from the
lofty altars of cloud.

Book Lover Pieta

Passing through the room
where my hardworking husband
lies on the old couch with a book,
I am stopped by the shape
he makes floating in the lap
of his mother love: reading.

His free arm lays long
and slack over his belly,
his large veined hand
protecting his soft parts,
his head thrown back
as in laughter or release.

The middle finger of his other
hand is jammed into the thick
crease of the page he arrived at
before sleeping, which he does
now, balancing the open book
without any effort at all.

The Marvelous
for Jeff

Like the best gifts, hardly expected,
this dream awakens me to Us.

For the first time it is clearly you, my Love
who joins me in a dream, both of us

looking upward in a huge, darkened shell
that seems to float at the top of the world.

A million bright constellations move overhead,
yet it is merely a lightbulb we reach to change.

Oh, but within the lightbulb is one marvelous insect:
a small, opalescent creature suspended within a blue orb,

unattached and hovering perfectly, speaking to us,
offering undying love, even as we trade this magic

for a more worldly connection with light,
resting in the blackness between stars.

Magic Act

Only a gesture, the brush
of my skirt is enough to bring
you and your sidekick center stage.
No white rabbits here, but only the white
of sheets that entertain us, or the white
of sunlight pushed through a tree's
limbs, quivering. Awake instantly
as any shell creature to the sun,
your watery stem fills itself up.
Like a wand used expertly I watch it,
your baton of flesh not quite linear.
I take in the curve of you amazed
at this perfect edifice your body
has imagined will do the trick.
This is the magic act that transfixes
and you fix me good where I am broken,
arching upward that which leaned
precariously low, supporting the point
within me that wants to bounce.
With innate timing and grace you come
over me like a wave over sand, pushing
a thick strand of seaweed with the gentle
weight of you, bending as the strong
cord of green bends and bobs, afloat.
We are the shadow we make moving
on the wall, both of us suspended
by the wand that flourishes and arcs
toward the earth herself,
toward her horizon
and her vapors.

No Matter What

When you act small,
I grow to twice my normal size.
When you suddenly expand,
I become a cricket, repeating
a song known only to me.

Like clockwork we make this exchange
over and over until the day we awake
and celebrate a new holiday:
tell the truth no matter what.

A thousand great love poems
get translated into every language
and are released around the globe.

Doors open outward, and windows open in.

Size and frequency don't matter
or being perfect,
or being right.

The new day dawns crisp
and clear. My cricket song gains
full power and fills our bedroom
with small *ahhs* and whispers of joy.

Eros

Not sleeping, but smoking Camels
at the kitchen table while
everyone else sleeps.
Not sleeping when I should
because I should. Baking cookies
at midnight because at midnight
the smell of baking chocolate
is just for me. Not sleeping,
like slipping out the back door
in the middle of the night
when I was thirteen because snow
covered everything, made the night
as light as a gray winter day.
Walking alone, scaring myself,
inventing crisp conversations
between characters who are all me
not sleeping but remembering sleep,
making love to my first boyfriend
like I make a God out of the painter
who smudges my electric blue leggings
with white. Not sleeping, but dreaming,
swirling sea water in a teacup. Painting
a small table and chairs black. Lighting
white candles, almond incense,
the gas oven, dousing everything
with light and scent. Burning my
hand on the stove. Washing
black panties in cold water.
Not sleeping but constructing
metaphors for sleep. Eating
cookie dough, but not the
cookies. Making patterns for
children's pants out of newspaper.
Cropping photographs. Writing
letters to Congress. Washing dishes
silently. Not sleeping but wanting to.
Pouring sour milk down the drain.
Putting the cat on top of the refrigerator.
Listening to my boys talking in their sleep.
Folding clean, warm clothes, avoiding

the hot snaps. Not sleeping, but seeing
the backyard in Idaho, the fence Dad
build when I was sixteen, that same
summer mowing the front lawn
under the streetlight, entranced
by the slice of the push mower's blade
dicing the red and orange nasturtiums.
Falling off the front steps after my first,
real kiss. Paul Hernandez. Not sleeping
but remembering every bed I've ever
slept in, the over soft, the hard floors,
sleeping bags, men with braided hair,
women with large breasts. Sleeping
on the Interstate sandwiched between
children in disposable diapers. Sleeping
with my mother when dad was away
negotiating with the CWA in Denver,
her snore keeping me awake, amused.
Not sleeping, but alert, waiting, trying
to forget the wind that ripped across
my childhood. Waiting to grow up.
Retracing my stoned footprints
through the City of Rocks, hitchhiking
under stars unafraid, down roads lined
with gophers, mile markers, rusted
railroad ties. Walking toward the
faint sound of country music.
Not sleeping but looking months
ahead, planning my private life,
my great escape to Cape Cod,
the winter sun setting on
Herring Cove Beach, Race Point
far off and shrouded in mist,
my bearded lover with a fishing
pole and a grin, drinking vodka,
smelling of linseed oil and paint.
Not sleeping, but wanting sex,
an unfamiliar tongue, Eros incarnate,
the taste of red meat and red wine.
Listening to the fog horn in
Provincetown, Massachusetts,
and hearing it in Eugene, Oregon.

Listening for that wind that rages
off the Atlantic, but hearing
only rain falling steadily into the
Willamette Valley, running in
rivulets down my roof. Sending
my lover a towel for Christmas.
Not sleeping, but needing sleep.
Blowing out candles that leave
the smell of someone's birthday
in the air. Telling my sad husband
I love him, whispering into his sleeping
ear. Sleeping, but not sleeping well.
Believing I have become the Tooth Fairy
I am pushing the calcified fragments
of my children's teeth into potted plants.
Hiding cookies from them. Hiding new
packs of cigarettes from my husband.
Brushing dirt and twigs from my cat's
fur. Drinking cold milk from the carton.
Leaving the heat set on High. Folding
crisp twenty dollar bills into an old
honey jar. Sitting still in the dark,
lying down in the light. Sleeping
but forgetting how to sleep.
Forgetting nothing.

As If

we could consider this place
we touch in lovemaking

like a marketing proposal
or a bank loan

as if a sky filled with large
and puffy clouds *is* heaven

as if a parent's love is perfect
or a child's love is perfect

as if you discovered *you* were perfect
fashioned after a Goddess and dropped
onto the lap of Mother Earth

as if you were issued a key
to a box and realized
you *were* the box

as if you opened yourself
and found that even perfection
isn't really.

Cecil Brunner Roses

They came on first in spring,
bunches, flowering and falling
as pink snow onto the wet
blackness of the earth.
Late summer now,
a few determined clumps
continue to pour forth,
their petals rusty and limp
in the dry heat.
I am struggling awake,
a deep grief returning
a piece of dream:
one of the baby pink roses
grows from under the hood
of my clitoris, sweet and small.
Assured of my passing,
I ache for the tight bud,
the bloom and decay,
the long day with its' trick,
this short life.

Transformation

Black Walnut trees in full summer dresses
tremble in a sudden wind, tossing and pressing
inward, each leaf shimmering with heat.

They sigh and sing songs of useless regret
falling heavy on me in my ignorant grief.

Baked in the sun, the hard black nuts will fall
and go unused, my pale skin will turn brown.

I think of how the wind will arrive
to mark the passing of a great soul,
and I invoke the wind to witness
our failed romance,

our chance evaded and now
gone, as this green season
will surely go.

She Left

On the night she died,
the moon rose huge and full,
a wind storm coming up
from nowhere, the power out
all over southern Idaho.

Miles away, the candles
on my altar burned bright
as if she were right there.

I heard my voice
saying over and over
it's ok for you to go

The beating of my heart
returned me to the place
where I grew inside her
awaiting my descent
into this world.

I felt the wings of death
as they opened for her,
her soul moving forward
buoyed on tongues of flame
shining and singing

go, go, go

Heirlooms

> *for my brothers and sisters*

I have figurines now because
my mother had them and I couldn't
let them go into the auction boxes:
the goose girl in green,
the twin child musicians,
a porcelain egg with a red Robin
feeding her young that's inscribed
Every Spring is a New Beginning.

The goose girl is my favorite,
an old friend from childhood.
She holds three bright eyed
goslings in a basket on her arm,
the other hand reaching down
to the elegant goose standing
at her feet, a pointed slipper
of russet red peeking out
from her glorious green skirt.

The boy twin plays an accordion,
a red bow tie and soft green jacket
a bit dressy with his black shorts
and bare, pink legs. His sister sports
an oversized, turquoise bow atop
her blond head, her orange skirt
revealing bloomers, ruffled and white.

The porcelain egg cracks me open.
The Robin *is* my mother who always
called us her chicks, blessing each
with unwavering faith even as she left us,
these talismans of joy and simple beauty
the glowing lanterns along a dark road.

Loss

Since mom died my 86 year old father
says he's ready to *cash in his chips,*
kick the bucket, meet his maker
because living is too painful.

Meanwhile his grown children, no longer
young ourselves and also grieving
are working hard to keep our hearts
open, hopeful, but for what?

Maybe he could decide to stay,
take up a new hobby or perhaps
a lover that will interest him
more than *buying the farm?*

I want him to know
we still need him to be *here*
for *us,* that we haven't given up
on his life just yet.

But in the light of his longing
to *get his ticket punched* our needs
collapse, these coarse phrases
his gift for making friends with loss.

Surviving November

Lay down, stand naked
as trees revealing their bones
black against cloud masses
nowhere to hide your secrets
come clean, stand naked
the wind doesn't care
laying back our soft parts
ragged growth overgrown
color drained of color
black white gray
no place for hiding
animal needs howling
excess opening wide
eat too much drink too much
the wind doesn't care
heavy rains come and come
stand naked, bones revealed
old wounds opening up
chimes falter and clang
heavy rains come and come
rise up in your skeleton
lay down in your bones
music turning your ragged edges
to mush, mush the gray light
dull the naked light dripping
clanging chimes wake you up
damn chimes put you to sleep
music dying away, loving
the little deaths, revealing
your darkest truths
stand naked, let bones sing
desire hot in your heart
the wind doesn't care.

Moss in Winter

Love, you and your sister Death
are a set of insatiable twins.

One's countenance becomes blurred
and the other relieves you, calling

and calling into the weakening light, saying
goodbye but meaning only goodnight.

You blot each other out, woo us, and leave us
to our bitters, our personal drugs.

In Love, Death is a green cloak
enshrouding the dream field,

while at Death's little door, the memory
of the Lover divides and covers everything.

Is this soft bed of moss deadly I ask,
beating my palms on tree bark,

evoking the spirits of the beloved
to blame them, for closing forever

the wounds that would have healed us.

Sleeping Girl With a Cat

after the painting by Auguste Renoir

The old painter hired this girl
turned sleepy and limp toward
the light of the sun, a cat's paw
caught on one hand and forearm.
Her other hand catches the blue
folds of her skirt as if in dream.
She sleeps with the concentration,
the weighted heart of a worker:
her eyebrows taut, her lips
with a slight part, her heavy
shoes flat to the wooden floor.
The dried flowers of her cap
sprinkle their dust onto her
white shoulder, relieved for now
of a whiter chemise, her breasts full
keeping the light garment
from falling clear away.
With her own magic she floats,
anchored deep in the armless
red chair that buoys her up,
the stowaway cat purring
deep in her blue lap,
asleep.

What the Cat Doesn't Know

I would love to teach my cat
to brush and floss,
it would be so much better
for the vet bill, and really
I think he'd actually enjoy it.

He can open his mouth so wide
and cleans the rest of himself
so thoroughly, it would be a new
pleasure, a bit more domestication
to improve his already robust health.

I picture his furry little chin
foaming with toothpaste,
his fangs exposed and scrubbed—
though perhaps spitting might be
problematic—*Can a cat do that?*

I believe his deft paws could easily
maneuver the floss, sharp claws holding
and dragging it perfectly between each
pointed tooth like he now grooms his
whiskers, wondering what's on my mind.

Mercy Killing

When you began to curl
into yourself, a perfect circle
of orange fur from tail to the
tips of your keen ears, I knew
your time to go was near.

I couldn't look you in the eye,
and not because of your sores
but because my heart quaked,
made a sound in my chest
I hoped you couldn't hear.

Four adults in a cramped room
with you trembling and afraid
and the decision was made,
enclosing each of us in clarity
and the will to end your life.

Merciful, but still a killing,
an untimely ending imposed
without your full consent, our best
intentions no comfort to me now,
my duty to you satisfied, but cold.

Winter Solstice

We pour out our pockets late at night,
see the endings for the beginnings
they are, moving from bed to stove,
from stove to bed as if
toward places of worship.

As if we were children,
and we are, we play a game
called sleep with the darkness,
our expectations marked
by candles carefully lit and placed.

The hours, like gloved fingers
push us through the narrowing eye
of a needle, our fibrous bodies
cold, yet not indifferent, many
stranded and difficult to squeeze
through such a narrow passageway.

As if we were angels,
and we are, we play a game
called patience with this season,
bearing ourselves toward Spring
with a child's vengeance, that
sheer will we were born with.

We kneel on quilted edges
waiting for the world to turn,
for the sun to strike us
square in the face,
daring joy.

IV

Spring Snow

The dense quiet,
then the glow
that brightens
the sky
even at 2AM.

The Angel
of the Intricate
Snowflake has
touched down,
softening
every edge,
quiet and sneaky with
her saving Grace.

Pink and pink-white
flowering fruit trees
will bend and break
under her weight.

Water will run
in the streets like
small rivers, bounding
over the broken limbs.

But right this minute
she is light of step
and whispering
into my sleeping ear:

awaken.

Driving West

Crossing over the Cascades
my car climbs the narrow
road up through a forest
recently burned but still
standing, light reaching the
ground where light has been
rare, burnt stumps scattered
and giving way to lava beds,
acres of chunky black rock
beaten up by weather,
the fluctuations of extreme
heat and extreme cold
over time, now stretching
to a ragged horizon line,
tight hallways bored between
sharp stone, the empty road
narrowing more and more
as an ancient memory
of the birth canal rises
within me, pressing
my worldly body up
and out as I summit,
and then finally begin
the long descent down
and down into the folded
valley I call home, bending
and curving my torso,
my long arms with each
turn in the smooth road,
looping and falling through
a forest of green and gold,
a blur of light and trees
that accept me
just as I am.

Creekside

If you find yourself
lucky enough to be creekside
let the creek creek you.

Open your ears completely
and let the gurgling water
water you.

Allow the dappled light
to dapple your sight
until light shimmers you.

Feel the trickle of water
tickle you, all your thoughts
falling away into that bright void.

Let the breeze breeze you, the trees
tree you, the great old Fir standing by
be the only witness to your surrender.

Let the water that keeps
arriving and arriving
arise in your center,

until only light and wonder
at being right here
remains.

Even the Bees

are languid in their busy work.

The begonia persists in her red
velvet loveliness, but the peach one
is undone, falling over the edge
of her pot with sweet abandon.

The sunflowers droop and yawn,
their heavy heads dripping seed
and forward thinking thoughts,
bowing low to the bounty
of the vegetable garden.

The hours stretch open
before me like long, warm arms
filled with gratitude, quiet, repose.

Who Tends the Garden?

The *Whirling Butterflies* have twirled
their stems like a hurricane beating
back the less determined flowers:
Penstemon, Hollyhocks, Poppies.

The Shasta daisies go off like fireworks
sprawling white and bobbing in wind,
at night glowing bright in the dark.

Strawberry plants grow long tentacles
charging down footpaths oblivious
to feet and river rock borders.

Bright pink tulips pop up
in odd places, the handiwork
of squirrels who have their own
agendas, who shake the feeder
until all the seed is gone
or scattered or both.

Chattering birds drop from the trees
and disappear. The untended leggy roses
tower up through vigorous trumpet vine
dropping their deep red petals one at a time.

The despised and stubborn Bindweed
spirals around everything growing skyward:
weed or flower, flower or weed,
entwined.

Sonnet for Patience

What's to become of us
when our passions turn pale
and what we have left of lust
is balanced on the body's scale?
Your shoulder that won't turn
a certain way, my lower back
that longs to sway and burn
but comes up short, a tender lack.
Our bones and years are measured
side by side, our deepest desires
better in memory and treasured,
the kindling for small, secret fires.
I will plant myself with the bright seed
of patience, an aspiration beyond need.

A Late Fall This Year

the earth turning
faster than the leaves
sticking stubbornly to trees,
or drifting about aimlessly
as usual.

The wine grapes stayed green,
then ripened quickly,
prey to migratory birds
working fast to catch up
with time.

Rotted blossoms cling
to each other, torrid
oranges and hot pinks
bobbing in late afternoon light
almost light hearted, but not.

Harvest

If the hour of this day
could stand in for the
year I am living now
I would guess it's about
four-thirty, or maybe
just four twenty-seven,
since it can't hurt to push
back time for the sake
of this poem.

It's too late for a bracing
cup of black tea, too early
for red wine. My kitchen
counters are piled high
with apples and green pears,
poems and books stacked up
in small towers on my desk.

Old memories are cracked open
by simple chores done well:
weeding and canning, crushing
flowers while a solid blue sky
looks on, the vegetable garden
growing all by itself, the arms
of tree branches dancing
wildly in a hot wind.

Planting Garlic

The black soil glistens
in late afternoon light. It could
be Spring, but it's the waxing
moon of October, a warm breeze
blowing in from the south.

The garlic skins flutter purple
and gleaming white from my hands:
Nootka Rose, Inchelium Red and Purple Glazer—
the cloves easily peeled and revealing
moist pearls of fragrant gold.

Arranged in circle patterns
like crocodile teeth, or bits of shell,
my thumb finds each and pushes it down
just like I was taught, or taught myself
this art of hope in spite of winter.

First Snow

Crisscrossing snowflakes
dance in the air like birds.

Mocha brown Mourning Doves
coo and cluster under the feeder,

their pale breasts and under feathers
revealed as they flutter upward

to bounce on tree limbs,
relieving them of weight

and making their own flurries
of sifted, white powder.

The Towhees ask why, the Crows know,
the Doves huddle together for warmth.

My Child My Nemesis

Arguing with you
is like arguing
with myself
only worse.
We're too smart
for each other,
too smart for our
own good and we
go to the darkest
corners fast.

I know when I've
been insulted and
so do you. We can't
hide from each other
or this torment we make
over and over again,
a torrent of sharp words
zigzagging around
and past each other
like mad birds.

We both dismiss peace
and refuse surrender
until we reach utter
exhaustion or tears,
laying open our
broken hearts
like raw meat
before a fire.

When I ask myself
Is this really love
I already know
the answer, and
it isn't the one
I thought I wanted.

Forgiveness

Disappointment
is a cracked jar
that will not hold water.

Break this jar
and watch
your heart open.

Will the jar be completely mended
or brought back to full use?

No, but the heart will.

We're All in This Together
for Saramaria

We circle our chairs under
summer trees, the air blowing hot
and then cool, filtering through
the dappled green of leaves,
growing still with expectation.

You've been trying out for the role
of the bad daughter for a long time,
long enough that you believe
completely in your viewpoint
but no longer want the part.

I am bombing in my role
as the reluctant step mother
standing in the wings like a ghost,
not sure of my entrance line
or my deep motivations.

Your father cues off our silences,
his words wandering in circles
around old wounds:
*the tone of a text, the bad
Thanksgiving, his depression
era parents who couldn't say
I love you.*

I wish I could gather all of us
into an airy basket for curing,
letting the masks and shields
of our character studies fall away
like husks we no longer need.

The Circle

When someone we love
leaves this world
we are invited to stand
inside the circle
of eternity
for a little while.

From this vantage point
all perspective tilts
toward the inevitable,
and a large window
opens onto a field
that beckons us.

We know that someday
we will follow and a deep
pulling on the heart
begins to rearrange
and allow us to see
just how things are.

This is a circle for
hand holding and love
surrendered with tears,
a glimpse of the truth
that we finally only exist
for one another.

Acknowledgments

"Ultrasound Odalisque" was published by the *Atlanta Review*.

"The Jewel" was published in *Lactuca* and *From Here We Speak: An Anthology of Oregon Poetry*.

"My Boy" was published in *The Sow's Ear*.

"Opening and Closing", "Sieves" and "Provincetown" (formerly titled "Looking for Someone") were all published by the *Silverfish Review*.

"August" and "Clouds" appeared in *Mudfish 5*.

"Eros" was published by *Calypso*.

About Atmosphere Press

Atmosphere Press is an independent, full-service publisher for excellent books in all genres and for all audiences. Learn more about what we do at atmospherepress.com.

We encourage you to check out some of Atmosphere's latest releases, which are available at Amazon.com and via order from your local bookstore:

Until the Kingdom Comes, poetry by Jeanne Lutz

Warcrimes, poetry by GOODW.Y.N

The Freedom of Lavenders, poetry by August Reynolds

Convalesce, poetry by Enne Zale

Poems for the Bee Charmer (And Other Familiar Ghosts), poetry by Jordan Lentz

Serial Love: When Happily Ever After… Isn't, poetry by Kathy Kay

Flowers That Die, poetry by Gideon Halpin

Through The Soul Into Life, poetry by Shoushan B

Embrace The Passion In A Lover's Dream, poetry by Paul Turay

Reflections in the Time of Trumpius Maximus, poetry by Mark Fishbein

Drifters, poetry by Stuart Silverman

As a Patient Thinks about the Desert, poetry by Rick Anthony Furtak

Winter Solstice, poetry by Diana Howard

Blindfolds, Bruises, and Break-Ups, poetry by Jen Schneider

Songs of Snow and Silence, poetry by Jen Emery

INHABITANT, poetry by Charles Crittenden

Godless Grace, poetry by Michael Terence O'Brien

March of the Mindless, poetry by Thomas Walrod

In the Village That Is Not Burning Down, poetry by Travis Nathan Brown

Mud Ajar, poetry by Hiram Larew

To Let Myself Go, poetry by Kimberly Olivera Lainez

I Am Not Young And I Will Die With This Car In My Garage, poetry by Blake Rong

photo by Robert Consentino

DM Wallace was born and raised in a large Catholic family in Twin Falls, Idaho where she first started writing poetry in high school. She has lived in Eugene, Oregon all of her adult life where she raised two sons and completed a degree in Communications and Film at the University of Oregon.

Making her living in the wine business and as a water aerobics instructor, she lives and gardens with her husband Jeff and her two cats Lillikoi and Lenore.

www.ingramcontent.com/pod-product-compliance
Lightning Source LLC
Chambersburg PA
CBHW032122050726
47590CB00008B/2930